The Complete New York Times Thanksgiving Cookbook

Full of Recipes That'll Make Your Pants Too Tight

BY

Jaxx Johnson

∘O——O○O——O∘

License Page

Table of Contents

Introduction

Welcome to your new favorite cookbook! This book is like a friendly chat with your neighbor over the fence, sharing all those yummy recipes that make mouths water and tummies happy. We've packed these pages with classic American dishes that have been filling plates and warming hearts for generations.

From grandma's secret meatloaf to that apple pie that always wins at the county fair, we've got it all. But don't worry - we're not just throwing a bunch of ingredients at you and saying "good luck!" Nope, we're walking you through each recipe step by step, just like a good friend would.

You'll find dishes for every part of the meal - snacks to nibble on while you're cooking, main courses that'll make the family rush to the table, sides that could steal the show, and desserts that'll have everyone asking for seconds (or thirds!).

We've kept things simple and straightforward. No fancy chef lingo here - just good, honest cooking that anyone can do. Whether you're just starting out in the kitchen or you've been cooking for years, you'll find something here to love.

This book is perfect for those busy weeknight dinners, lazy weekend brunches, holiday feasts, and everything in between. It's not just about following recipes - it's about creating memories around the dinner table, sharing laughs, and enjoying good food with the people you care about.

So roll up your sleeves, tie on that apron, and get ready to cook up some magic. These recipes are tried, tested, and guaranteed to bring smiles to faces and warmth to hearts. Let's get cooking!

Appetizers

1. Cheesy Bacon Mushroom Bites

This English dish is a hit at parties. People love it because it's easy to make and tastes great. The main ingredients are mushrooms, bacon, and cheese. You'll enjoy the mix of flavors and textures. It's a perfect snack or appetizer for any occasion.

Preparation Time: 15 minutes

Cooking Time: 30 minutes

Serving size: 2

Ingredients:

- 4-6 medium-large portobello mushrooms
- 4 oz unsmoked bacon lardons
- 4 tbsp dried breadcrumbs
- 1 shallot, finely chopped
- 1 garlic clove, finely chopped
- 1 tsp dried sage
- 1/2 cup grated medium cheddar

Instructions:

a. Turn on your oven to 425°F. Clean the mushrooms and take out the stems.
b. Put them upside down on a baking sheet.
c. Cook the bacon in a pan until it's almost crispy. Chop up the shallot, mushroom stems, and garlic really small. Add them to the bacon and cook for about 5 minutes until everything looks done.
d. Take the pan off the heat. Mix in the breadcrumbs and sage. Stir it all together.
e. Fill the mushrooms with this mixture. Sprinkle cheese on top.
f. Bake for 8-10 minutes until the cheese melts. Serve with bread and salad.

Special Notes:

- Try soaking the mushrooms in red wine for 30 minutes before cooking. It adds a nice flavor twist.

- For a vegetarian version, swap the bacon for chopped nuts like walnuts or pecans. It'll give a similar crunchy texture.

2. Cheesy Wands

These crunchy cheese sticks are from the UK. People love them as snacks or party food. They're made with flour, butter, and cheddar cheese. You'll enjoy their crispy texture and savory taste. They're easy to make and hard to resist!

Preparation Time: 10 minutes

Cooking Time: 20 minutes

Serving Size: 4

Ingredients:

- 2/3 cup all-purpose flour
- 3&1/2 tbsp unsalted butter, cold and cubed
- 1/2 cup shredded cheddar cheese
- 4 tsp cold water
- 1/4 cup whole wheat flour
- 1/2 tsp mustard powder

Instructions:

a. Set your oven to 400°F. Get a baking sheet ready with some oil or parchment paper.

b. Mix the flours and mustard powder in a bowl.

c. Add the cold butter cubes to the flour mix. Use your fingers to mash it all together until it looks like breadcrumbs.

d. Toss in the shredded cheddar and mix it up.

e. Slowly add cold water while stirring with a knife. Keep going until you have a nice, smooth dough.

f. Dust your work surface with a bit of flour. Roll out the dough into a rectangle about 1/5 inch thick.

g. Neaten up the edges, then cut the dough into thin strips about 1/2 inch wide and 3 inches long.

h. Put these strips on your prepared baking sheet.

i. Bake for about 10 minutes. They're done when they turn a nice golden brown color.

Special Notes:

- For extra crunch, try sprinkling some sesame seeds on top before baking. Just be careful if anyone has seed allergies!

- Want to spice things up? Mix in a pinch of smoked paprika with the flour for a subtle smoky flavor that pairs great with the cheese.

3. Shrimp Party Dip

This Shrimp Party Dip is an old favorite from the US. It's a hit at gatherings and easy to make. You'll need big shrimp and a tangy sauce. It's cold, fresh, and tasty - perfect for hot days. Once you try it, you'll want to make it again and again.

Preparation Time: 15 minutes

Cooking Time: 20 minutes

Serving size: 4

Ingredients:

Poaching Liquid:

- 2 cloves garlic, peeled and squashed
- 2 sprigs fresh tarragon
- 12 cups cold water
- 1/4 onion, sliced
- 1/2 lemon
- 1 tbsp seafood seasoning (like Old Bay®)
- 1 tsp whole black peppercorns
- 1 bay leaf

Cocktail Sauce:

- 1/2 cup ketchup
- 1/4 cup prepared horseradish
- 1 tsp lemon juice
- 1 tsp Worcestershire sauce
- 3 drops hot sauce, or to taste
- 1/4 cup chili sauce
- 1 pinch salt

Shrimp:

- 2 pounds shell-on deveined jumbo shrimp

Instructions:

a. Mix water, onion, tarragon, garlic, seafood lemon, seasoning, peppercorns, and bay leaf in a big pot. Heat it up until it's just about to boil. Let it sit for 15 minutes to mix the flavors.

b. In a bowl, mix ketchup, chili sauce, horseradish, lemon juice, Worcestershire sauce, hot sauce, and salt. Put it in the fridge to cool down for at least 15 minutes.

c. Now, get the pot boiling fast. Throw in the shrimp and cook until they turn pink and aren't see-through in the middle. This takes about 5 minutes. Then, quickly put the shrimp in a bowl of ice water to cool them down. Once they're cold, drain the water.

d. Put the cold shrimp on a plate and serve with the cool sauce you made earlier.

Special Notes:

- For extra flavor, add a splash of white wine to the poaching liquid. It gives the shrimp a subtle, fancy taste.

- Try grilling the shrimp instead of boiling for a smoky twist. Just brush them with oil and cook for 2-3 minutes per side on a hot grill.

4. Classic Deviled Eggs

These classic deviled eggs are a hit at parties. They're easy to make and taste great. People love them because they're creamy and flavorful. The recipe comes from the southern US and uses simple ingredients like mayo and mustard. You'll want to make them again and again.

Preparation Time: 35 minutes

Serving size: 4

Ingredients:

- 6 large eggs
- 1 tsp white vinegar
- 1/8 tsp salt
- 1/4 cup mayonnaise
- 1 tsp yellow mustard
- Ground black pepper to taste
- Smoked Spanish paprika for topping

Instructions:

a. Put eggs in a pot with cold water. Make sure there's 1.5 inches of water above the eggs. Turn the heat to high. When it boils, cover the pot and lower the heat. Cook for 1 minute. Take the pot off the heat but keep it covered for 14 minutes. Then run cold water over the eggs for 1 minute.

b. Peel the eggs under cool water. Pat them dry with paper towels. Cut each egg in half the long way. Scoop out the yolks into a bowl. Put the white parts on a plate. Mash the yolks with a fork until they're smooth. Mix in the mayo, vinegar, mustard, salt, and pepper.

c. Spoon the yolk mix back into the egg whites. Use about a tsp for each. Sprinkle paprika on top before serving.

Special Notes:

- For extra creamy yolks, push them through a fine mesh strainer before mixing with other ingredients.

- Try adding a dash of hot sauce to the yolk mixture for a spicy kick that'll surprise your guests.

5. Spinach Cheese Bites

These small tarts are from Italy. People love them as snacks or party food. They're made with spinach and cheese in a flaky crust. You'll like how the creamy cheese mixes with the green spinach. They're easy to make and taste great hot or cold.

Preparation Time: 20 minutes

Cooking Time: 26 minutes

Serving size: 24

Ingredients:

- 10 oz Panela cheese
- 10 oz Cotija cheese
- 1 large egg
- 2 premade pie crusts
- 2 tbsp butter
- 1 medium onion, diced
- 1 garlic clove, minced
- 1 tsp salt
- 8 cups spinach

Instructions:

a. Turn on the oven to 375°F. Get a 24-count mini or 12-count regular cupcake pan ready. Roll out the pie crusts a bit thinner. Cut circles bigger than the cupcake cups. Put the dough in the cups and press it down with a shot glass.

b. Melt butter in a big pan. Cook onion and garlic until see-through, about 5 minutes. Add salt and spinach to the pan. Cover it to help the spinach shrink. Cook until the water's gone.

c. Let the spinach mix cool a bit. Break up both cheeses into small bits.

d. Mix cheeses, spinach stuff, and egg in a big bowl.

e. Fill each dough cup with the mix. Don't push it down.

f. Bake big ones for 26-28 minutes, small ones for 20-22 minutes. They're done when the crust looks golden.

g. Let them sit in the pan for 5 minutes. Then move them to a rack to cool more.

Special Notes:

- For extra crunch, sprinkle some breadcrumbs on top before baking.

- Try swapping spinach for kale or Swiss chard for a different taste. Just make sure to cook out all the water first.

6. Oyster Delight

This dish was created in New Orleans in 1899. It's a hit at fancy parties. You'll need oysters, spinach, and cheese. The rich, creamy topping on fresh oysters will make your mouth water. It's perfect for special dinners or when you want to show off your cooking skills.

Preparation Time: 30 minutes

Cooking Time: 30 minutes

Serving size: 16

Ingredients:

- 48 fresh oysters, unopened
- 1 package (10 oz) frozen chopped spinach, thawed and drained
- 2 cups (8 oz) Monterey Jack cheese, shredded
- 2 cups (8 oz) fontina cheese, shredded
- 2 cups (8 oz) mozzarella cheese, shredded
- 1&1/2 cups beer
- 1/2 cup (4 oz) unsalted butter
- 1 onion, chopped
- 1 clove garlic, crushed
- 1/2 cup milk
- 2 tsp salt, or to taste
- 1 tsp ground black pepper
- 2 tbsp fine bread crumbs
- 2 cloves garlic
- 7 black peppercorns
- Seasoned salt to taste

Instructions:

a. Wash the oysters well. Put them in a big pot with beer, water (enough to cover), 2 garlic cloves, peppercorns, and seasoned salt. Bring to a boil, then turn off the heat.

b. Drain and let cool. Heat your oven to 425°F (220°C).

c. When the oysters are cool, take off the top shells and throw them away. Put the oysters on a baking sheet.

d. In a pan, melt the butter over medium heat. Cook the onion and crushed garlic until soft. Turn the heat down and add spinach and all the cheese.

e. Stir until the cheese melts. Add milk, salt, and pepper.

f. Put some of this mix on each oyster, filling the shell. Sprinkle bread crumbs on top.

g. Bake for 8-10 minutes until the top is golden and bubbly.

Special Notes:

- For extra flavor, add a splash of Pernod or any anise-flavored liqueur to the spinach mixture.

- If you can't find fresh oysters, you can use pre-shucked ones. Just skip the boiling step and place them directly on rock salt in a baking dish before topping.

7. Cranberry Mixer

This tangy cranberry salsa comes from the American Southwest. It's a hit at parties and potlucks. The mix of tart cranberries, spicy jalapeño, and zesty lime gives it a kick. You'll love how it goes with chips, tacos, or grilled meats. It's easy to make and always gets people talking.

Preparation Time: 15 minutes

Cooking Time: 15 minutes

Serving size: 6

Ingredients:

- 12 oz fresh cranberries
- 1 bunch cilantro, chopped
- 3/4 cup white sugar
- 1 medium jalapeño pepper, seeded and minced
- 1 bunch green onions, cut into 3-inch lengths
- Juice of 2 medium limes
- 1 pinch salt

Instructions:

a. Grab your food processor and fit it with the medium blade.
b. Toss in the green onions, cranberries, cilantro, sugar, and jalapeño.
c. Squeeze in the lime juice and add a pinch of salt.
d. Put the lid on and pulse the mixture. Keep going until everything's chopped up but still a bit chunky. Don't turn it into mush!
e. Taste it. Need more kick? Add more jalapeño. Too tart? Throw in a bit more sugar.
f. That's it! Your Red Zinger is ready to rock.

Special Notes:

- Secret tip: Add a splash of orange juice for a sweeter twist. It balances out the tartness nicely.

- Quirky trick: Try mixing in some diced mango. The sweetness pairs well with the cranberries and gives the salsa a tropical vibe.

8. Baked Brie

This fancy cheese appetizer is a hit at parties. It's from France and lots of people love it. You wrap Brie cheese and cranberry sauce in puff pastry and bake it. It's warm, gooey, and tasty. The sweet and tangy cranberry goes great with the soft cheese.

Preparation Time: 25 minutes

Cooking Time: 35 minutes (plus 1 hour chilling)

Serving size: 8

Ingredients:

For the Baked Brie:

- 1 (10 to 12 oz) round Brie cheese
- 1 sheet puff pastry (from a 17.3 oz package), thawed if frozen
- 1/2 cup Cranberry Chutney (cooled to room temperature)
- 1 large egg, beaten
- All-purpose flour, for dusting

For the Cranberry Chutney:

- 1 (12 oz) bag fresh or frozen cranberries
- 1 Granny Smith apple, grated
- 1/2 tsp ground ginger
- 1 pinch ground cloves
- 1/2 cup sugar
- 1/2 tsp ground cinnamon
- Zest and juice of 1 orange
- Salt and black pepper to taste

Instructions:

a. Heat your oven to 400°F. Put some parchment paper on a baking sheet.

b. Cut the Brie in half like a hamburger bun.

c. Spread the Cranberry Chutney on the bottom half. Put the top back on.

d. Roll out the puff pastry on a floured surface.

e. Make it 3-4 inches bigger than the Brie all around. Put the Brie in the middle.

f. Cut an inch off each corner of the pastry. Save these bits for decorating if you want. Fold the corners to the middle of the Brie. Brush some egg where they meet.

g. Fold the rest of the edges to wrap up the Brie.

h. Flip the wrapped Brie onto the baking sheet, seam-side down. Decorate the top if you like. Put it in the fridge for an hour.

i. Bake for about 35 minutes until it's golden brown. Let it cool for 10 minutes before moving it to a plate.

For the Cranberry Chutney:

a. Mix cranberries, apple, sugar, spices, orange zest and juice, and 1/4 cup water in a pot. Boil it.

b. Turn the heat down and cook for about 20 minutes until it's thick. Add salt and pepper how you like it.

Special Notes:

- For extra flavor, mix some chopped rosemary into the cranberry chutney before spreading it on the Brie.

- If you're short on time, you can skip the chilling step. Just pop it in the freezer for 15 minutes instead for a quick chill that'll help the pastry keep its shape while baking.

9. Squash Soup Surprise

This soup comes from Italy. It's a favorite fall dish that many people enjoy. The main star is butternut squash, mixed with herbs and spices. You'll love how smooth and tasty it is. It's perfect for cold days when you want something warm and filling.

Preparation Time: 10 minutes

Cooking Time: 35 minutes

Serving size: 6

Ingredients:

- 1 (3-pound) butternut squash, peeled, seeded, and cubed
- 3 to 4 cups vegetable broth
- 1 tbsp chopped fresh sage
- 2 tbsp olive oil
- 1 large yellow onion, chopped
- 1/2 tbsp minced fresh rosemary
- 1/2 tsp sea salt
- 1 tsp grated fresh ginger
- 3 garlic cloves, chopped
- Black pepper, freshly ground

For serving:

- Toasted pepitas
- Crusty bread
- Chopped parsley

Instructions:

a. Get a big pot and put it on medium heat. Pour in the oil. Toss in the onion and sprinkle salt and pepper. Cook until the onion gets soft, about 5-8 minutes.

b. Add the squash cubes and keep cooking for 8-10 minutes. Stir now and then.

c. Now, throw in the garlic, sage, rosemary, and ginger. Stir for about a minute until you can smell all the good stuff. Pour in 3 cups of broth. Turn up the heat until it starts bubbling. Then, put a lid on it, turn down the heat, and let it simmer.

d. Cook until you can easily poke the squash with a fork, about 20-30 minutes.

e. Let the soup cool a bit. Then, pour it into a blender. You might need to do this in batches if your blender is small. Blend until it's smooth. If it's too thick, add more broth, up to 1 cup. Taste it and add more salt or pepper if needed. Serve it up with parsley, pepitas, and some bread on the side.

Special Notes:

- Secret flavor boost: Try roasting the squash before adding it to the pot. It'll give the soup a deeper, nuttier taste.

- Quirky twist: Swap half the squash for sweet potatoes. It'll add a new layer of flavor and a pretty orange color to your soup.

10. Nutty Medley Munchies

This nut mix comes from the Southern US. It's a hit at parties and game nights. The nuts are cooked with maple and spices. You'll love how the sweet and spicy flavors mix. It's easy to make and great for snacking.

Preparation Time: 10 minutes

Cooking Time: 15 minutes

Serving size: 6

Ingredients:

- 1/2 cup pecans
- 1/2 cup almonds
- 1/3 cup pistachios
- 1/3 cup cashews
- 1/3 cup pumpkin seeds
- 1 tbsp maple syrup
- 1/2 tsp curry powder
- 1/8 tsp cayenne pepper
- 1/2 tsp dried rosemary
- 1/4 tsp salt
- Cooking spray

Instructions:

a. Turn on the oven. Set it to 325°F.
b. Get a bowl. Put all the nuts and seeds in it.
c. Add the maple syrup, spices, and salt to the bowl. Mix everything well.
d. Spray some cooking spray on a baking sheet.
e. Put the nut mix on the baking sheet. Spread it out in one layer.
f. Put the baking sheet in the oven. Cook for 15 to 20 minutes.
g. Halfway through, take out the baking sheet. Stir the nuts. Put it back in.
h. When done, the nuts should smell good and look a bit darker.

Special Notes:

- Try adding a pinch of smoked paprika for a smoky twist.

- For a sweet-and-salty kick, sprinkle some sea salt flakes over the nuts right after they come out of the oven.

Mains

11. Turkey Pot Pie

This Turkey Pot Pie is a tasty way to use up leftover turkey. It's a simple dish that comes from American home cooking. Many folks make it after Thanksgiving. The main ingredients are turkey, veggies, and a flaky crust. You'll love how comforting and filling it is.

Preparation Time: 40 minutes

Cooking Time: 40 minutes

Serving size: 6

Ingredients:

- 2 cups leftover turkey, diced or shredded
- 1/4 cup all-purpose flour
- 2 cups low-sodium chicken or turkey broth
- 1 pie crust (homemade or store-bought)
- 1/4 cup butter
- 1/2 cup finely diced onion
- 1/2 cup finely diced carrot
- 1/2 cup finely diced celery
- 3/4 cup heavy cream
- 2 tsp fresh thyme, chopped
- 1/4 cup white wine (optional)
- 1 cup frozen peas (optional)
- Salt and pepper to taste

Instructions:

a. Heat your oven to 400°F.

b. Melt the butter in a big pan. Toss in the onion, carrots, and celery. Cook until they're soft.

c. Add the turkey and mix it in. Sprinkle flour over everything and stir well. Keep cooking and stirring for a couple of minutes.

d. Pour in the broth, stirring as you go. If you want, add the wine now. Then pour in the cream. If you like peas, throw them in too.

e. Let it bubble gently and thicken up for a few minutes. Add salt, pepper, and thyme. Taste it and add more of what it needs.

f. Pour the mix into a baking dish.

g. Roll out your pie crust so it's a bit bigger than your dish.

h. Put the crust on top of the filling. Tuck the edges into the sides of the dish. Cut some slits in the top.

i. Bake for 30-40 minutes. It's done when the crust is golden and the filling is bubbling.

j. Let it cool a bit before you dig in.

k. Serve it up with a big spoon.

Special Notes: For extra flavor, try adding a splash of Worcestershire sauce to the filling. It gives a nice savory kick. Also, if you have any leftover roasted veggies, chop them up and toss them in. They'll fit right in and add more yummy bits to your pie.

12. Maple Orange Chicken

This chicken dish comes from New England. It's a hit at family dinners. The recipe mixes maple syrup and orange juice to make the chicken taste sweet and tangy. You'll love how the skin gets crispy and how the meat stays juicy. It's easy to make and tastes great with the roasted veggies.

Preparation Time: 20 minutes

Cooking Time: 2 hours 30 minutes

Serving size: 4

Ingredients:

- 2 cups chicken broth
- 20 fingerling potatoes
- 20 baby carrots
- 1 whole chicken (6-8 pounds)
- 1/4 cup olive oil
- 1 whole garlic head, top cut off
- 1/2 cup maple syrup
- 1/2 cup orange juice
- 1 whole shallot, top cut off
- Zest of 2 oranges
- Sea salt

Instructions:

a. Heat your oven to 400°F.

b. Clean the chicken and pat it dry. Put the potatoes and carrots in a big pot or pan. Place the chicken on top. Stuff the garlic, shallot, and orange pieces inside the chicken. Tie the legs with string. Rub oil all over the chicken. Sprinkle on the orange zest, salt, and pepper. Cook for 30 minutes.

c. Mix orange juice, maple syrup and 1 cup broth in a bowl.

d. Pour 1 cup of this mix into a measuring cup.

e. Add the rest of the broth to the bowl.

f. After 30 minutes, pour 1 cup of syrup over the chicken. Turn the oven down to 375°F. Cook for 45 more minutes, then pour the rest of the mix over the chicken. Keep cooking for about 1&1/2 hours. The skin should be brown and crispy. Check that the inside is 165°F to 180°F. If it's browning too fast, cover it with foil.

g. Take the chicken out and let it rest for 15 minutes.

h. For gravy, melt 2 tbsp butter in a pan. Add 2 tbsp flour and mix. Pour in 2 cups of the juice from the pan. Heat and stir until it's smooth.

i. Put the chicken and veggies on a plate. Cut it up. You can pour some of the maple orange mix on top. Serve the gravy on the side.

j. Dig in and enjoy!

Special Notes:

- Try adding a splash of bourbon to the maple-orange glaze for a grown-up twist. It adds a nice smoky flavor that goes well with the sweet and tangy notes.

- For extra crispy skin, pat the chicken dry and let it sit uncovered in the fridge for a few hours before cooking. This dries out the skin, helping it get super crispy in the oven.

13. Chestnut Sage Bread Mix

This bread mix with chestnuts and sage brings the forest to your table. It's a hit at Thanksgiving dinners across America. The mix of chestnuts, herbs, and bread makes a tasty side dish. It goes well with turkey and gravy. You'll love how the flavors blend together.

Preparation Time: 15 minutes

Cooking Time: 40 minutes

Serving size: 8

Ingredients:

- 10 cups day-old white bread, cut into 1/2-inch cubes
- 2 tbsp fresh parsley, chopped
- 1 tbsp fresh thyme, chopped
- 2 large eggs, beaten
- 2 1/2 cups vegetable stock
- 4 tbsp unsalted butter (2 oz), plus extra for greasing
- 1 small onion, chopped
- 2 celery stalks, chopped
- 3 garlic cloves, minced
- 2 tbsp fresh sage, chopped
- 1 tsp kosher salt
- 1 tsp ground black pepper
- 1&1/2 cups cooked chestnuts, roughly chopped

Instructions:

a. Heat your oven to 375°F. Grease a 9x13-inch dish with butter.

b. Melt butter in a big pan. Cook onion and celery until soft, about 5-7 minutes.

c. Toss in garlic. Cook for 1 minute. Don't let it burn.

d. Add sage. Cook for 1 minute more. Take the pan off the heat. Let it cool for 5 minutes.

e. In a big bowl, mix bread cubes, parsley, and thyme.

f. Add eggs, stock, salt, pepper, and the cooked veggies to the bowl. Mix lightly.

g. Gently stir in the chestnuts.

h. Put the mix in the greased dish. Spread it out evenly. Press it down a bit.

i. Bake for 35-40 minutes until the top is light brown.

j. Let it cool for a few minutes before serving.

Special Notes:

- Try toasting the bread cubes in the oven before mixing. It gives them a nice crunch.

- For a twist, add some dried cranberries. They bring a sweet-tart pop that goes great with the chestnuts.

14. Stuffed Pork Roast

This stuffed pork roast is a hit at family dinners. It's from the American South, where cornbread is king. The mix of pork and cornbread stuffing is tasty and filling. It's not hard to make, but it looks fancy. You'll love how the flavors come together.

Preparation Time: 1 hour 15 minutes

Cooking Time: 1 hour 5 minutes

Serving size: 6

Ingredients:

- 8 oz ground Italian pork sausage
- 2 lb. pork loin
- 2 cups crumbled cornbread
- 1 tsp fresh sage leaves, chopped
- 1 tsp fresh thyme leaves, chopped
- 1/4 cup grapeseed oil, divided
- 1 small onion, diced
- 1 tsp fresh parsley leaves, chopped
- 2 egg whites
- 1/4 cup heavy cream
- 3 tbsp butter, melted
- Salt and black pepper to taste

Instructions:

a. Heat 2 tbsp oil in a big pan. Cook onions until see-through. Add sausage and cook until it's no longer pink, about 5 minutes. Mix in cornbread and herbs. Cook 3-4 more minutes. Let it cool down.

b. Once cool, fold in whipped egg whites, cream, and melted butter. Add salt and pepper to taste.

c. Cut the pork loin to unroll it flat. Spread the stuffing on top. Roll it back up and tie with string every 1-2 inches. Chill for an hour.

d. Heat oven to 400°F. In a big pan, heat 2 tbsp oil and brown the pork all over. Put the pan in the oven for 15-17 minutes. Lower heat to 350°F.

e. Check the pork after 10 minutes. Take it out when it reaches 135°F inside. Cover with foil and let it rest for 5 minutes. It'll keep cooking to 145°F.

f. Slice and serve on a big plate.

Special Notes:

- For extra flavor, rub the outside of the pork with a mix of garlic powder, paprika, and dried oregano before searing.

- If you like a bit of sweetness, add a handful of dried cranberries to the stuffing mix. It'll give a nice pop of flavor and color.

15. Herby Butter Turkey Roast

This turkey roast comes from American kitchens. It's a hit at Thanksgiving and other big meals. The bird gets rubbed with herbed butter, which makes it super tasty. You'll love how the meat turns out juicy and flavorful. It's a crowd-pleaser that's easier to make than you might think.

Preparation Time: 30 minutes

Cooking Time: 3 hours 45 minutes

Serving size: 10

Ingredients:

- 1 turkey (10-12 pounds)
- 1 stick (8 tbsp) unsalted butter, soft
- 1 tbsp fresh chives, minced
- 2 lemons, cut into quarters, plus 2 tsp lemon juice
- 1&1/2 tsp fresh flat-leaf parsley, minced, plus 3 sprigs
- Salt and black pepper
- Pinch of cayenne pepper

Instructions:

a. Take the turkey out of the fridge. Let it sit for about an hour to warm up.

b. Heat your oven to 400°F. Take out the giblets from the turkey. Cut off any extra fat. Dry the turkey with paper towels. Add salt and pepper inside and out.

c. Mix the soft butter, chives, lemon juice, minced parsley, cayenne, 1/2 tsp salt, and 1/2 tsp pepper in a bowl. Loosen the turkey's skin over the breast. Push half the butter mix under the skin. Rub the rest all over the outside. Put the lemon quarters and parsley sprigs inside the turkey. Tie the legs with string. Tuck the wings under. Put the turkey on a rack in a roasting pan, breast side up.

d. Cook until the turkey starts to turn golden, about 25 minutes. Cover the breast loosely with foil. Turn the oven down to 325°F. Keep cooking until the thigh is about 155°F inside. Take off the foil and cook until the thigh hits 165°F, about 30 minutes more. Move the turkey to a cutting board and let it rest for 30 minutes.

e. Before you cut it, take out the lemons and parsley from inside.

Special Notes:

- For extra crispy skin, pat the turkey dry and leave it uncovered in the fridge overnight before cooking. This dries out the skin, helping it crisp up nicely in the oven.

- Try adding a couple of crushed garlic cloves to the herb butter mixture. It'll give the turkey an extra punch of flavor without overpowering the other herbs.

16. Easy Salmon Bake

This salmon dish is a no-fuss meal that's big on taste. It's from the Pacific Northwest, where salmon is king. People love it because it's quick to make and has lots of veggies. You'll like how the fish turns out tender and full of flavor. It's great for a family dinner or when you have friends over.

Preparation Time: 10 minutes

Cooking Time: 30 minutes

Serving size: 6

Ingredients:

- 1&1/2 pounds wild salmon
- 1 blood orange (or valencia orange), thinly sliced
- 1/4 cup fresh chives, chopped
- 1&1/2 pounds carrots
- 1/2 cup fresh dill, lightly chopped
- 1 lemon, thinly sliced
- 2 tbsp olive oil
- 2 tsp kosher salt
- 1 &1/2 tsp freshly ground black pepper
- 2 tbsp capers with brine
- 1&1/2 cups peas

Instructions:

a. Heat your oven to 425°F. It needs to be nice and hot to start.

b. Get your carrots ready. Cut them into big sticks. Put them in a large baking dish. Now, add half the dill, half the lemon slices, and half the orange slices. Pour in 1 tbsp of olive oil, 1 tsp of salt, and 3/4 tsp of pepper. Don't forget the capers! Mix it all up. Pop it in the oven for about 12-15 minutes. You want the carrots to start getting soft.

c. Take the dish out and turn the oven down to 375°F. Toss the peas in with the carrots. Now, place your salmon on top of all those veggies. Drizzle the rest of the olive oil on the fish. Sprinkle the remaining salt and pepper. Finish by putting the rest of the dill on top.

d. Back in the oven it goes! Cook until the salmon reaches 120°F inside. This should take about 15-20 minutes. Once it's done, let it sit for 10 minutes before you serve it. Sprinkle those fresh chives on top right before you eat.

Special Notes:

- Try adding a splash of white wine to the veggie mix before baking. It'll give a nice zing to the dish.

- If you're not a fan of dill, try using fresh basil instead. It'll change the flavor profile but still taste great with the salmon and veggies.

17. Honey Ham Spectacular

This ham recipe is a hit at family gatherings. It's from the American South and everyone loves it. The main stars are a big ham and a sweet honey glaze. You'll go crazy for the mix of salty meat and sugary coating. It's perfect for holidays or when you want to impress your guests.

Preparation Time: 10 minutes

Cooking Time: 3 hours

Serving size: 2

Ingredients:

- 1 (8-10 pound) bone-in, spiral-cut ham, no added water or juices
- 2 cups light brown sugar, packed
- 2 tbsp unsalted butter
- 2 tbsp apple cider vinegar
- 1 cup honey
- 1/2 cup Dijon mustard

Instructions:

a. Set your oven to 275°F. Put two long pieces of foil in a roasting pan, making sure they're big enough to wrap around the ham.

b. Take the ham out of its package. Put it in the pan with the cut side down. Wrap the foil around it tightly. This keeps the ham juicy while it cooks.

c. Cook the ham for about 2 to 2.5 hours. Check it after 1.5 hours. It's done when a meat thermometer stuck in the middle (not touching the bone) reads at least 120°F.

d. While the ham cooks, make the glaze. Put all the other ingredients in a pot on medium-high heat. Stir it often so the sugar doesn't clump. When it starts bubbling, turn the heat down. Let it cook for about 20 minutes until it gets thicker and darker. Take it off the heat when it's done.

e. When the ham has about 30 minutes left, take it out and unwrap it. Brush the warm glaze all over, getting it between the slices if you can. Put it back in the oven without the foil on top.

f. Cook for about 30 more minutes. It's ready when the thermometer reads between 120°F and 140°F.

g. Take the ham out and let it sit for 5-10 minutes. Then, cut around the bone and along the fat lines to separate the slices.

Special Notes:

- For extra flavor, stick some whole cloves into the ham before you cook it. Just remember to take them out before serving!

- If you like a bit of tang, add a tbsp of orange zest to the glaze. It gives a nice citrusy kick that goes great with the sweet honey.

18. Prime Rib Feast

This prime rib roast is a hit at family dinners. It's popular in steakhouses and home kitchens across America. The main star is a big chunk of beef, seasoned with herbs and garlic. You'll love how it turns out tender and full of flavor. It's perfect for special occasions or when you want to treat yourself.

Preparation Time: 10 minutes

Cooking Time: 1 hour 45 minutes

Serving size: 10

Ingredients:

- 5 lbs. of beef prime rib.
- 8 cloves garlic, minced
- 2 tsp black pepper, ground
- 2 tsp rosemary, fresh
- 1 tsp thyme, fresh
- 1/4 cup olive oil
- 2 tsp sea salt
- Horseradish for serving (optional)

Instructions:

a. Take the prime rib out of the fridge an hour before cooking. Sprinkle salt all over it and cover it loosely with plastic wrap. Let it sit on the counter to warm up.

b. Move the oven rack so it's in the middle. Heat the oven to 500°F.

c. Mix 1 1/2 tsp salt, pepper, thyme, rosemary, garlic, and olive oil in a small bowl.

d. Dry the meat with paper towels. Rub the seasoning mix all over it. If your roast has bones, put it in a roasting pan with the bones down. If it doesn't have bones, put it on a rack in the pan.

e. Cook the prime rib at 500°F for 15 minutes. Then turn the heat down to 325°F and keep cooking until it's done how you like it. Use a meat thermometer to check:
   - Rare: 120°F (about 10-12 min/pound)
   - Medium Rare: 130°F (about 13-14 min/pound)
   - Medium: 140°F (about 14-15 min/pound)
   - Medium Well: 150°F

f. Take it out of the oven when it's 5-10 degrees below where you want it. It'll keep cooking while it rests.

g. Take the roast out and cover it with foil. Let it sit for 30 minutes.

h. Cut the meat against the grain into slices about 1/2 inch thick. Serve with horseradish if you want.

Special Notes:

- For extra flavor, crush some whole peppercorns and press them onto the meat before cooking. It gives a nice crust and a bit of spice.

- If you like, you can add a cup of beef broth to the bottom of the pan. It'll make a tasty sauce to pour over the meat when you serve it.

19. Mushroom Log Surprise

This vegan twist on the classic Wellington comes from the UK. It's a hit at dinner parties. Portobellos and walnuts make it meaty and rich. You'll love how the crispy pastry contrasts with the soft filling. It's easier to make than it looks!

Preparation Time: 30 minutes

Cooking Time: 1 hour 5 minutes

Serving size: 6

Ingredients:

- 15 oz puff pastry sheets (1 package)
- 8 portobello mushrooms
- 1/2 cup olive oil
- 1 garlic clove, minced
- 1 sprig fresh rosemary, leaves removed
- 1 tbsp fresh thyme leaves
- 2 tbsp fresh sage, chopped
- 1 cup walnuts
- 1 medium onion
- Salt to taste
- Black pepper to taste

Instructions:

a. Heat your oven to 390°F with the fan on.

b. Put 5 mushrooms in a baking pan. Sprinkle it with salt and pepper. Pour 2 tbsp olive oil on top. Flip them over and do the same on the other side.

c. Bake for 15 minutes.

d. Turn the oven down to 375°F, still using the fan.

e. Chop up the other 3 mushrooms and throw them in a food processor.

f. Add garlic, 3 tbsp olive oil, salt, pepper, rosemary, thyme, sage, and walnuts to the processor. Blend until you get a paste.

g. Heat up a frying pan with 1 tbsp olive oil.

h. Roughly chop the onion and fry it for 1-2 minutes until it starts to brown.

i. Add the mushroom paste to the pan. Cook on medium for 15 minutes, stirring often. You want most of the liquid to cook off.

j. Roll out the puff pastry on your counter.

k. Spread half the cooked mushroom mix on one side of the pastry. Layer the whole mushrooms on top, then cover with the rest of the mix. Roll it up like a log. Dab some water on the edge to seal it.

l. Move the log to a baking sheet lined with parchment. Brush 1 tbsp olive oil on top.

m. Bake for 40-50 minutes until golden brown.

n. Let it cool for a few minutes before slicing and serving.

Special Notes:

- For extra flavor, soak dried porcini mushrooms in hot water for 30 minutes. Chop them up and add to the paste mixture.

- If you're not strictly vegan, brush the pastry with beaten egg instead of olive oil for a glossier finish.

20. Veggie Lasagna Stack

This veggie lasagna is a hit at potlucks. It's packed with mushrooms, zucchini, and bell peppers. People love its cheesy layers and rich tomato sauce. It's an Italian American favorite that's perfect for family dinners or when you have guests over. You'll enjoy how the flavors blend together.

Preparation Time: 20 minutes

Cooking Time: 45 minutes

Serving size: 8

Ingredients:

- 15 oz ricotta cheese (or 2 cups small curd cottage cheese)
- 2 &1/2 cups grated mozzarella cheese, divided
- 1/2 cup grated Parmesan cheese, divided
- 2 &1/2 cups store-bought (or homemade) marinara sauce
- 9 oven-ready, no-boil lasagna noodles
- 2 tsp olive oil
- 8 oz sliced mushrooms
- 1 medium zucchini, diced
- 1 sweet bell pepper (any color), seeded and diced
- 1 small onion, diced
- 1 tbsp minced fresh garlic (about 3 cloves)
- 1 large egg, beaten
- 2 tbsp chopped fresh parsley (or 2 tsp dried parsley flakes)
- 2 tbsp chopped fresh basil (or 2 tsp dried basil)
- Salt and black pepper, to taste
- Optional: chopped fresh herbs for garnish (parsley or basil)

Instructions:

a. Heat your oven to 400°F. Grease a 9x13-inch baking dish.

b. In a big pan, heat the oil. Toss in the mushrooms, zucchini, bell pepper, onion, and garlic. Cook until they're soft, about 3-5 minutes. Add some salt and pepper.

c. In a bowl, mix the egg, parsley, basil, ricotta, 1 ¼ cups mozzarella, and ¼ cup Parmesan.

d. Stir the marinara sauce into the cooked veggies.

e. Spread a thin layer of the veggie-sauce mix in the baking dish. Top with 3 noodles, then ⅓ of the cheese mix, then ¼ of the sauce mix.

f. Do this two more times.

g. Sprinkle the rest of the mozzarella and Parmesan on top.

h. Cover with greased foil. Bake for 35 minutes.

i. Take off the foil. Bake 5-10 minutes more until it's hot and the cheese is brown.

j. Let it sit for 10 minutes before you cut it. Add fresh herbs on top if you want.

Special Notes:

- Try adding a handful of spinach leaves between layers for extra nutrition and a pop of green.

- For a crunchy top, mix breadcrumbs with melted butter and sprinkle over the cheese before the final bake. It adds a nice texture contrast to the soft layers.

Sides

21. Mac 'n' Cheese Comfort Bowl

]This old-school Mac 'n' Cheese recipe is a hit in many homes. It's easy to make and tastes great. The creamy cheese sauce and soft pasta make it a go-to meal for both kids and adults. You'll love how quick and yummy it is.

Preparation Time: 10 minutes

Cooking Time: 15 minutes

Serving size: 4

Ingredients:

- 2 cups shredded Cheddar cheese
- 8 oz elbow macaroni
- 2 cups whole milk
- 1/4 cup unsalted butter
- 1/4 cup all-purpose flour
- 1/2 tsp salt
- Ground black pepper to taste

Instructions:

a. Get a big pot of water boiling. Add some salt. Throw in the macaroni and cook it for 8 minutes. You want it soft but still a bit firm when you bite it.

b. While the pasta's cooking, grab a saucepan. Melt the butter over medium heat.

c. Once the butter is melted, add the flour, salt, and pepper. Mix it up until it's smooth. This should take about 5 minutes.

d. Now, slowly pour in the milk. Keep stirring the whole time. Cook and stir until it's smooth and starts to bubble. This takes about 5 minutes. Watch it closely so the milk doesn't burn.

e. Time for the cheese! Add the Cheddar and stir until it's all melted. This should take 2 to 4 minutes.

f. Drain the cooked macaroni. Mix it into the cheese sauce until it's all covered.

g. Dish it up and dig in while it's hot!

Special Notes:

1. For extra flavor, try adding a pinch of smoked paprika to the cheese sauce. It gives a subtle smoky taste that many people love.

2. If you like a crunchy top, put the mac and cheese in a baking dish, sprinkle breadcrumbs on top, and pop it under the broiler for a few minutes until golden.

22. Creamy spinach

This creamy spinach dish is a hit in many homes. It's a simple side that goes well with almost any meal. The mix of soft spinach and rich sauce makes it tasty. You'll like how easy it is to make and how good it tastes. It's a great way to eat more veggies without trying too hard.

Preparation Time: 10 minutes

Cooking Time: 15 minutes

Serving size: 8

Ingredients:

- 3/4 cup whole milk
- 14 ounces fresh spinach
- 1/2 cup heavy cream
- 2 tbsp unsalted butter
- 1 small onion, finely chopped
- 2 tbsp all-purpose flour
- Fresh nutmeg, for grating
- Salt and pepper to taste

Instructions:

a. Melt the butter in a pot over medium heat.

b. Toss in the chopped onion and cook until it's soft, about 5 minutes.

c. Sprinkle the flour over the onions.

d. Stir and cook for 2 minutes to get rid of the raw flour taste.

e. Slowly pour in the milk, whisking as you go.

f. Keep stirring until the sauce gets thick, about 5 minutes.

g. While the sauce cooks, put the spinach in a big strainer.

h. Pour hot water over it to wilt the leaves. You might need to do this twice.

i. Squeeze out extra water from the spinach using a clean kitchen towel. Chop it up roughly.

j. Mix the spinach into the sauce. Pour in the cream and warm it up gently.

k. Add a bit of grated nutmeg, salt, and pepper. Taste and add more if needed.

Special Notes:

- Try adding a pinch of garlic powder to the sauce for extra flavor.

- For a twist, mix in some cooked, crumbled bacon just before serving. It adds a nice crunch and salty kick to the creamy spinach.

23. Buttermilk Biscuits

These buttermilk biscuits are a Southern staple. They're light, fluffy, and perfect for breakfast or as a side dish. Made with simple ingredients like flour, butter, and buttermilk, these biscuits are easy to whip up. You'll love their golden crust and soft, flaky insides.

Preparation Time: 20 minutes

Cooking Time: 15 minutes

Serving size: 12 biscuits

Ingredients:

- 2 cups all-purpose flour
- 7 tbsp unsalted butter, frozen and sliced thin
- 3/4 cup cold buttermilk
- 2 tsp baking powder
- 1/4 tsp baking soda
- 1 tsp salt
- 2 tbsp buttermilk for topping

Instructions:

a. Heat your oven to 425°F. Put a silicone mat or parchment paper on a baking sheet.

b. Mix the dry stuff in a big bowl - flour, baking powder, baking soda, and salt.

c. Add the frozen butter slices to the flour mix. Use a pastry cutter to chop it up until it looks like little pebbles.

d. Make a hole in the middle of the flour mix. Pour in the cold buttermilk and stir it around gently until it's just mixed.

e. Dump the dough onto a floured counter. Pat it into a rectangle shape.

f. Fold the dough like a letter, then turn it and flatten it again. Do this two more times.

g. Roll the dough until it's about 1/2 inch thick. Use a round cutter (about 2 1/2 inches wide) to cut out biscuits. You should get 12 total.

h. Put the biscuits on your baking sheet. Press your thumb into the top of each one to make a little dent.

i. Brush some buttermilk on top of the biscuits.

j. Bake for about 15 minutes until they're golden brown and flaky.

k. Take them out and enjoy your homemade biscuits!

Special Notes:

- For extra-flaky biscuits, freeze your butter, then grate it into the flour mixture instead of slicing it.

- Try adding a handful of shredded cheddar cheese to the dough for a savory twist. Or mix in some dried herbs like rosemary or thyme for a flavor boost.

24. Sweet Tater

This sweet potato casserole is a hit at holiday dinners. It's from the southern US and mixes sweet potatoes with a crunchy pecan topping. People love it because it's both sweet and savory. You'll want seconds for sure!

Preparation Time: 20 minutes

Cooking Time: 45 minutes

Serving size: 12

Ingredients:

Sweet Potato Mix:

- 4 cups sweet potatoes, peeled and cubed
- 4 tbsp butter, softened
- 1/2 tsp vanilla extract
- 1/2 tsp salt
- 2 large eggs, beaten
- 1/2 cup white sugar
- 1/2 cup milk

Pecan Topping:

- 1/3 cup all-purpose flour
- 1/2 cup brown sugar, packed
- 3 tbsp butter, softened
- 1/2 cup pecans, chopped

Instructions:

a. Heat your oven to 325°F. Get all your stuff ready.

b. Boil the sweet potatoes. Put them in a pot with water.

c. Cook until you can easily stick a fork in them, about 10-15 minutes. Drain the water out.

d. Mash the sweet potatoes in a big bowl. Mix in the eggs. Then add sugar, milk, butter, vanilla, and salt. Stir until it's smooth. Pour this into a 9x13-inch baking dish.

e. Now for the topping. In another bowl, mix the flour and brown sugar. Add the butter and mix it in with your hands until it looks like little peas. Don't mix too much. Stir in the pecans. Sprinkle this all over the sweet potato mix.

f. Bake for about 30 minutes. The top should look a bit brown.

g. Take it out and let it cool a bit before you dig in.

Special Notes:

- For extra flavor, try roasting the sweet potatoes instead of boiling them. It brings out their natural sweetness.

- If you're feeling fancy, swap out half the pecans for chopped bacon. It adds a salty crunch that goes great with the sweet potatoes.

25. Garlic Potato Mash

This garlic potato mash comes from the US. It's a hit at family dinners. You need potatoes, garlic, cream, and butter. The roasted garlic gives it a deep, rich taste. It's warm, smooth, and goes well with many main dishes. You'll love how easy it is to make.

Preparation Time: 5 minutes

Cooking Time: 40 minutes

Serving size: 6

Ingredients:

- 2 pounds Yukon Gold potatoes
- 1/2 tsp salt, plus extra for taste
- 1/3 cup heavy cream
- 3 tbsp butter
- 1 whole head of garlic
- 1 tbsp olive oil

Instructions:

a. Heat your oven to 400°F.

b. Get your garlic ready. Take off the papery outside skin, but keep the head in one piece. Cut off the top part of the cloves so you can see inside. Put the garlic on some foil, pour olive oil over it, add a bit of salt, and wrap it up. Cook it in the oven for 30 to 40 minutes until it's soft and starting to brown. Let it cool when it's done.

c. While the garlic's cooking, peel and chop your potatoes into 1-inch pieces. Put them in a pot with 1/2 tsp of salt and cover with cold water. Bring the water to a boil, then turn it down and let the potatoes cook for about 15 minutes. You'll know they're done when you can easily stick a fork in them.

d. In a small pot or in the microwave, warm up the cream and melt the butter together.

e. When the potatoes are cooked, drain the water and put the pot back on low heat. Add the potatoes back in. Squeeze the roasted garlic into the pot and start mashing everything together.

f. Pour in your warm cream and butter mixture. Keep mashing until you like how it looks. Don't overdo it or your potatoes might get sticky.

g. Taste it and add more salt if you think it needs it.

Special Notes:

- For extra flavor, try adding a splash of white wine to the cream and butter mixture before you warm it up. It gives the mash a subtle, tangy kick.

- If you want a smoother texture, use a ricer instead of a masher. It'll make your potatoes extra fluffy and lump-free.

26. Sage-Infused Cornbread Mix

This Southern-inspired dish puts a twist on classic cornbread. It's a hit at family gatherings and potlucks. The secret? Sage-infused butter that gives it a rich, herby taste. It's easy to make and goes well with many meals. You'll love how the crispy top contrasts with the soft inside.

Preparation Time: 20 minutes

Cooking Time: 45 minutes

Serving size: 8

Ingredients:

- 6 cups cornbread cubes (1-inch pieces), about 1 pound
- 3/4 cup water
- 2 large eggs, beaten
- 1 large Vidalia or Spanish onion, chopped (about 1 cup)
- 1/2 cup (1 stick) unsalted butter, divided
- 1/3 cup freshly picked sage leaves (about 12), stems removed
- Salt and black pepper to taste

Instructions:

a. Heat your oven to 375°F.

b. In a large pan, melt 2 tbsp butter over medium heat. Add the onion, salt, and pepper. Cook for 6–8 minutes, or until light gold. Put the sautéed onions on a platter.

c. Turn up the heat to medium-high. Add water to the pan. Let it bubble for a couple of minutes to soak up the onion flavor. Take the pan off the heat.

d. Put cornbread cubes in a big bowl. Melt the rest of the butter in a small pan. Let it bubble until it starts to turn golden. Toss in sage leaves and fry for 30 seconds. Use a slotted spoon to put the sage on the cornbread. It will get crispy there.

e. Pour the golden butter over the cornbread. Add eggs and cooked onions. Mix in salt and pepper. Slowly add the onion water, stirring gently. Add just enough to make the cornbread moist but not soggy.

f. Put the mix in a 9x11-inch baking dish. Bake for about 30 minutes. It's done when the top is golden and the middle is set.

Special Notes:

- Try adding a handful of dried cranberries to the mix. They'll give bursts of tartness that go great with the sage.

- For extra crunch, sprinkle some chopped pecans on top before baking. They'll toast up nicely and add a nutty flavor.

27. Green Bean Bake

This Green Bean Bake is a quick and easy American side dish. It's a hit at potlucks and holiday dinners. You'll love the mix of tender green beans and creamy mushroom sauce, topped with crispy onions. It's a tasty way to get your veggies and please the whole family.

Preparation Time: 5 minutes

Cooking Time: 30 minutes

Serving size: 6

Ingredients:

- 2 cans (15 oz each) cut green beans, drained
- 3/4 cup milk
- 1 can (2.8 oz) French fried onions
- 1 can (10.5 oz) condensed cream of mushroom soup
- Salt and pepper to taste

Instructions:

a. Turn on your oven and set it to 350°F. Get all your stuff ready.

b. Grab a medium-sized casserole dish. Dump in the green beans, mushroom soup, and milk. Add half of the fried onions. Mix it all up.

c. Pop the dish in the hot oven. Let it cook for about 25 minutes.

d. You'll know it's done when it's hot and bubbly.

e. Take the dish out. Sprinkle the rest of the fried onions on top.

f. Put it back in the oven for 5 more minutes.

g. Once it's out, add some salt and pepper if you want. Taste it first to see how much you need.

Special Notes:

- For extra crunch, crush some potato chips and mix them with the fried onions on top.

- If you like it cheesy, stir in a handful of shredded cheddar before baking. It'll make the dish even more comforting.

28. Bacon-Kissed Brussels Sprouts

This dish comes from the heart of American comfort food. It's a hit at dinner parties and family gatherings. The mix of crispy bacon and tender sprouts is hard to beat. You'll love how the maple syrup adds a touch of sweetness to balance the savory flavors.

Preparation Time: 15 minutes

Cooking Time: 35 minutes

Serving size: 4

Ingredients:

- 4 thick slices bacon, cut into 1-inch pieces
- 1 pound Brussels sprouts, cut in half
- 4 cloves garlic, smashed and roughly chopped
- 2 tbsp extra-virgin olive oil
- 1 tsp kosher salt, plus extra for taste
- 1/2 tsp freshly ground black pepper, plus extra for taste
- 1 tbsp maple syrup
- 1/2 medium to large yellow onion, chopped into 1/2-inch pieces
- 1 tsp apple cider vinegar, plus extra for taste
- 1/8 tsp red pepper flakes, plus extra for taste

Instructions:

a. Set your oven to 450°F.

b. Spread the bacon pieces on a baking sheet. Pop it in the oven for 5 minutes.

c. While the bacon's cooking, mix the Brussels sprouts, onion, garlic, olive oil, salt, and pepper in a bowl.

d. After 5 minutes, take out the baking sheet. Add the Brussels sprout mix. Stir everything together. Flip the sprouts so they're flat-side down.

e. Cook for 20 to 30 minutes. Halfway through, stir the veggies and turn the pan around. You want the bacon crispy and the sprouts soft and a bit charred. Pour on the maple syrup, mix again, and cook for a few more minutes until they're as crispy as you like.

f. Take the pan out of the oven. Sprinkle on the vinegar and red pepper flakes. Mix it up. Give it a taste (careful, it's hot!) and add more salt, spice, or vinegar if needed.

g. You can eat this hot, warm, or even at room temp. It's all good!

Special Notes:

- Try swapping the bacon for pancetta for an Italian twist. It adds a deeper, saltier flavor that pairs wonderfully with the sprouts.

- For a veggie version, skip the bacon and add some chopped, toasted nuts at the end. Pecans or walnuts work great and add a nice crunch.

29. Citrus Cranberry Blend

This cranberry sauce is a hit at holiday dinners. It's from New England, where cranberries grow. People love it because it's sweet and tangy. You need cranberries, oranges, and some spices. It's easy to make and tastes way better than canned sauce.

Preparation Time: 5 minutes

Cooking Time: 25 minutes

Serving size: 16

Ingredients:

- 12 oz fresh cranberries
- 1 tsp grated orange zest
- 1 cup orange juice
- 1/2 cup white sugar
- 1/2 cup brown sugar
- 1 tsp cinnamon
- 2 allspice berries

Instructions:

a. Mix juice, sugars, cinnamon, and allspice in a pot. Turn on medium heat.
b. Let it bubble for 5 minutes. Add cranberries. Cook and stir now and then until you hear popping sounds, about 10 minutes.
c. Throw in the orange zest. Keep cooking and stirring for 10 more minutes. Turn off the heat. Let it cool down and get thick.

Special Notes:

- Try adding a splash of vanilla extract at the end for a surprising twist.
- If you like it less sweet, swap half the white sugar with honey. It gives a nice flavor and cuts the sugar.

30. Autumn Veggie Medley

This vegetable dish comes from old European farms. It's pretty common nowadays. You'll need root veggies like beets and carrots. The maple and vanilla give it a nice sweet touch. It's great for fall dinners or holiday meals. You'll probably like how the different flavors mix together.

Preparation Time: 15 minutes

Cooking Time: 35 minutes

Serving size: 6

Ingredients:

Roasted Vegetables:

- 1-pound beets, peeled and chunked
- 2 large carrots, sliced into rounds
- 1-pound parsnips, peeled and chunked
- 1 small acorn squash, seeded and cubed
- 1 medium sweet potato, chunked
- 1 medium red onion, chunked

Maple Vanilla Butter:

- 2 tsp fresh rosemary, minced
- 2 tsp fresh sage, minced
- 2 tsp fresh thyme, minced
- 1/4 cup melted butter
- 2 tbsp maple syrup
- 1 tbsp vanilla bean paste
- 1/2 tsp sea salt

Crispy Herbs:

- 3 rosemary stems
- 1/4 cup olive oil
- 12 sage leaves

Instructions:

a. Turn on your oven to 425°F. Get two baking sheets and put parchment paper on them. Mix the maple vanilla butter stuff in a small bowl.

b. Put the beets and carrots on one sheet. Keep them apart if you don't want the beets to color the carrots. Pour 2 tbsp of the maple vanilla butter on them and mix it around. Cook for 30-35 minutes until they're soft and a bit golden on the edges.

c. On the other sheet, put the parsnips, sweet potato, red onion, and squash. Pour the rest of the maple vanilla butter on top and mix it up. Cook these for 20-25 minutes. Put this tray in the oven 10 minutes after the first one.

d. For the crispy herbs, put paper towels on a plate. Heat the olive oil in a small pan on medium. Fry the rosemary and sage leaves in small batches for about a minute until they're crispy. Put them on paper towels to cool off.

e. When everything's done, put all the veggies on a big plate and sprinkle the crispy herbs on top.

Special Notes:

- Try adding a splash of balsamic vinegar to the maple vanilla butter. It gives a nice tangy kick that goes well with the sweet stuff.

- If you want to make this dish even more colorful, throw in some purple potatoes or golden beets. They cook the same way as the other veggies and add more pretty colors to your plate.

Sweets

31. Tangy Fruit Wheel

This sweet and tart dessert comes from New England. It's a hit at fall gatherings. Cranberries and apples are the stars here. You'll love how the flavors mix in every bite. It's easy to make and always gets people talking.

Preparation Time: 15 minutes

Cooking Time: 35 minutes

Serving size: 16

Ingredients:

- 1 package (14 oz) double-crust pie pastry
- 2 medium tart apples, peeled and roughly chopped
- 2 cups cranberries, fresh or frozen, roughly chopped
- 1&1/4 cups brown sugar, packed
- 1/2 tsp ground cinnamon
- 1-2 tbsp butter
- 2 tbsp all-purpose flour

Instructions:

a. Roll out half the pastry on a floured surface into a 13-inch circle.
b. Press it into an 11-inch tart pan or 10-inch springform pan, covering the bottom and sides.
c. Mix cranberries, apples, brown sugar, flour, and cinnamon in a bowl.
d. Pour this mix into the pastry-lined pan. Add small chunks of butter on top.
e. Cut leaf shapes from the leftover pastry. Place these on the filling.
f. Put the pan on a baking sheet. Bake at 425°F for 35-40 minutes. The filling should bubble and the crust should turn golden.
g. Let it cool a bit, then serve warm.

Special Notes:

- Try adding a splash of orange juice to the fruit mix. It brings out the cranberry flavor.
- For extra crunch, sprinkle some chopped nuts on top before baking.

32. Silk-Smooth Chocolate Pie

This chocolate pie is a hit in many US homes. It's smooth, rich, and super chocolatey. People love it because it's easy to make but tastes like it took hours. The secret is in the mix of chocolate and whipped cream. Once you try it, you'll want to make it again and again.

Preparation Time: 20 minutes

Cooking Time: 5 minutes

Serving size: 8

Ingredients:

- 8 oz bittersweet chocolate, finely chopped
- 4 large eggs
- 2 cups heavy whipping cream
- 1/2 cup sour cream
- 1 cup plus 3 tbsp granulated sugar
- 3 tsp pure vanilla extract
- 3/4 cup unsalted butter, softened
- 1/4 tsp instant espresso powder
- 1 store-bought chocolate cookie crust
- A pinch of kosher salt

Instructions:

a. Mix the creams. Put the heavy cream, sour cream, 3 tbsp sugar, 1 tsp vanilla, and a tiny bit of salt in a big bowl. Beat it until it's thick and forms peaks. Split this mix in two and put it in the fridge.

b. Melt the chocolate. Put it in a bowl and zap it in the microwave. Do this in 30-second bursts, stirring each time, until it's smooth. Let it cool down.

c. Cook the eggs. Fill a pot with an inch of water. Put a bowl on top, making sure it doesn't touch the water. Mix eggs, the rest of the sugar, and a pinch of salt in this bowl. Heat the water and keep stirring the egg mix. Do this for about 10 minutes until it's pale and fluffy. It should be 160°F. Take it off the heat and mix in the rest of the vanilla and the espresso powder. Let it cool.

d. Beat the butter. Use a mixer to make it light and fluffy. This takes about 2 minutes. Then add the cooled egg mix and melted chocolate. Mix for 2 more minutes. Gently fold in half of the whipped cream you made earlier.

e. Fill the pie. Pour this mix into the pie crust. Smooth it out. Cover it lightly and put it in the fridge for at least 4 hours. When you're ready to eat, top it with the rest of the whipped cream.

Special Notes:

- For an extra kick, add a splash of your favorite liqueur to the filling. Baileys or Kahlúa work great!

- If you're in a hurry, pop the pie in the freezer for an hour instead of the fridge. It'll set faster, but don't forget about it or you'll end up with chocolate ice cream pie!

33. Classic Pumpkin Pie

This pumpkin pie is a staple at American holiday tables. It's loved for its smooth texture and warm spices. The main ingredients are pumpkin, condensed milk, and eggs. You'll enjoy the mix of sweet and spicy flavors in every bite. It's an easy-to-make dessert that's perfect for fall gatherings.

Preparation Time: 10 minutes

Cooking Time: 50 minutes

Serving size: 8

Ingredients:

- 1 can (15 oz) pumpkin puree
- 1 can (14 oz) sweetened condensed milk
- 1 (9 inch) unbaked pie crust
- 2 large eggs
- 1/2 tsp ground ginger
- 1/2 tsp ground nutmeg
- 1/2 tsp salt
- 1 tsp ground cinnamon

Instructions:

a. Turn on your oven and set it to 425°F.

b. In a bowl, mix pumpkin, milk, eggs, and spices until smooth.

c. Pour the mix into the pie crust.

d. Bake for 15 minutes at 425°F.

e. Lower the oven temperature to 350°F. Keep baking for 35-40 minutes.

f. Check if it's done by sticking a knife near the edge. If it comes out clean, it's ready.

g. Let the pie cool down before you cut it.

Special Notes:

- For a twist, try adding a pinch of black pepper to the spice mix. It gives a subtle kick that pairs well with the sweetness.

- If you like a firmer texture, swap out 1/4 cup of the pumpkin puree with mashed sweet potato. It'll give your pie a bit more structure without changing the flavor too much.

34. Apple Crumble

This apple crumble is a top pick for fall desserts. It's from the USA and is loved by many. The main stars are juicy apples and crunchy toppings. You'll enjoy the mix of sweet and tart flavors, perfect for a cozy night in or a family gathering.

Preparation Time: 15 minutes

Cooking Time: 1 hour 15 minutes

Serving size: 12

Ingredients:

For the filling:

- 3 pounds apples, quartered, cored, and sliced into 1/4-inch pieces
- 1 tbsp fresh lemon juice
- 1&1/2 tbsp cornstarch
- 1 tsp kosher salt
- 1/4 cup granulated sugar
- 2 tsp lemon zest
- 1 tsp ground cinnamon
- 2 tbsp Calvados (apple brandy) (optional)

For the streusel:

- 3/4 cup rolled oats
- 3/4 cup all-purpose flour
- 3/4 cup (1&1/2 sticks) unsalted butter, cut into 1/2-inch cubes
- 3/4 cup pecans, toasted and chopped
- 1/2 cup light brown sugar
- 1&1/2 tsp ground cinnamon
- 1/2 tsp allspice
- 1 tsp kosher salt

Instructions:

a. Heat your oven to 350°F. Grease a 9x9-inch baking dish.

b. Mix the apples, lemon zest, lemon juice, cornstarch, salt, sugar, and Calvados in a big bowl. Stir well to coat the apples and dissolve the cornstarch. Pour this mix into your greased dish. Sprinkle cinnamon on top.

c. For the topping, mix flour, oats, pecans, brown sugar, cinnamon, allspice, and salt in another bowl. Add the butter cubes and coat them with the dry mix. Use your fingers to work the butter in until you have pea-sized bits and it looks like wet sand.

d. Spread this topping evenly over the apples.

e. Bake for 55-75 minutes. You'll know it's done when the filling bubbles and the top is golden brown.

f. Let it cool for 30-40 minutes before serving. It should be just warm, not hot.

Special Notes: For an extra twist, try using a mix of apple types - some tart like Granny Smith and some sweet like Honeycrisp. This gives a more complex flavor. Also, if you don't have Calvados, a splash of vanilla extract can add depth to the filling without changing the classic taste too much.

35. Southern Nutty

This sweet treat comes from the American South. People love it during holidays. You'll find lots of pecans, sugar, and corn syrup in it. It's super sweet and nutty. If you like desserts that are rich and gooey, you'll enjoy this pie.

Preparation Time: 10 minutes

Cooking Time: 50 minutes

Serving size: 16

Ingredients:

- 12 large eggs
- 4 cups granulated sugar
- 4 cups light or dark corn syrup
- 6 cups pecan halves
- 4 (9-inch) unbaked deep-dish pie crusts (regular or gluten-free)
- 1 cup unsalted butter, melted
- 4 tsp vanilla extract

Instructions:

a. Turn on your oven and set it to 350°F.

b. Grab a big bowl. Crack the eggs into it and mix them up a bit.

c. Now, add the sugar, corn syrup, melted butter, and vanilla. Mix everything until it's all combined.

d. Get your pie crusts ready. Pour the mixture you just made into them. Make sure it's even.

e. Take your pecans and spread them on top of each pie. Use about 1 1/2 cups for each one.

f. Put the pies in the oven. Let them bake for 50 to 55 minutes.

g. When they're done, take them out and let them cool down on a wire rack.

h. Once they're cool, put them in the fridge to store.

Special Notes:

- Want a twist? Try toasting the pecans before adding them to the pie. It brings out a nuttier flavor that'll make your taste buds dance.

- If you're feeling adventurous, add a splash of bourbon to the filling. It gives the pie a grown-up kick that pairs wonderfully with the sweet, nutty flavors.

Conclusion

Well, folks, there you have it! You've just flipped through a treasure trove of tasty treats and hearty meals that'll keep your kitchen buzzing and your family's tummies happy. From appetizers that'll kick off any party right, to main dishes that'll become your go-to favorites, to desserts that'll have everyone asking for the recipe – you're now armed with a whole bunch of delicious possibilities.

Remember, cooking is all about having fun and making things your own. So don't be afraid to play around with these recipes. Add a pinch of this, a dash of that – who knows, you might just stumble upon your own secret family recipe!

We hope these pages have brought back some fond memories of meals shared with loved ones, and that they'll help you create new memories around your own dinner table. Whether you're whipping up a quick weeknight dinner or preparing a holiday feast, you've got all the tools you need right here.

So tie on that apron, roll up those sleeves, and get ready to fill your home with the wonderful smells of good cooking. And hey, if something doesn't turn out quite right the first time, don't sweat it! That's all part of the adventure.

Thanks for letting us be a part of your kitchen adventures. Now go on and cook up some happiness – your taste buds (and your lucky dinner guests) will thank you!

Author's Afterthoughts

Did you like my book? I pondered it severely before releasing this book. Although the response has been overwhelming, it is always pleasing to see, read or hear a new comment. Thank you for reading this and I would love to hear your honest opinion about it. Furthermore, many people are searching for a unique book, and your feedback will help me gather the right books for my reading audience.

Thank You!

Jaxx Johnson

Made in the USA
Monee, IL
14 October 2024

6ff9dbbf-f02e-4663-af87-806a2c9b5a2aR01